Today's Weather Is...
A Book of Experiments

by Lorraine Jean Hopping
Illustrated by Meredith Johnson

To Dr. Nora
—L.H.E.

It's never a rainy day
with Chris and Kaylyn
—M.J.

All of these experiments have been tested and retested with children and are known to be safe. However, it is always a good idea to have an adult present when children are performing experiments.

Text copyright © 2000 by Lorraine Jean Hopping
Illustrations copyright © 2000 by Meredith Johnson

For information contact:
MONDO Publishing
980 Avenue of the Americas
New York, New York 10018
Visit our website at www.mondopub.com

Printed in China
07 08 09 10   9 8 7 6 5 4 3

Design by David Neuhaus/NeuStudio

Library of Congress Cataloging-in-Publication Data
Hopping, Lorraine Jean.
  Today's weather is--: a book of experiments / by Lorraine Jean Hopping ; illustrated by Meredith Johnson.
    p. cm.
  ISBN 1-5722-809-1 (pbk.)
  1. Weather--Experiments--Juvenile literature. [1. Weather—Experiments. 2. Experiments.] I. Johnson, Meredith, ill. II. Title.

QC981.3 .H67 2000
551.6'078—dc21
                                                    00-042374

Contents

Chapter 1: Heat Islands   page 4
Experiments: Chocolate Melt and Hot-Air Spinner

Chapter 2: A Wind-Powered School   page 10
Experiments: Wind Flappers and Breezy Bubbles

Chapter 3: Catching Fog   page 16
Experiments: Fog in a Bottle and Jet Clouds

Chapter 4: Lightning Sparkers   page 22
Experiments: Homemade Lightning

Chapter 5: Iceberg Harvest   page 26
Experiments: Melt-a-thon and See-through Cubes

A Few Words About Weather   page 32

Chapter 1

Heat Islands

New York, NY—Big cities are islands of heat. They are often warmer than the area all around them.

What turns a city into a heat island? Lots of people and lots of people-made things such as cars.

People make body heat. Your body stays around 98.6°F (37°C). That is usually a lot warmer than the temperature outdoors.

All the cars, lights, and other machines in a city make heat, too. Feel the back of a TV set while it's on. Warm, isn't it?

Cities also have roads, sidewalks, and buildings. Those surfaces absorb, or keep in, much of the sun's heat. Plants, dirt, rivers, and lakes absorb less heat.

Most cities also have smog, or polluted air. Smog acts like a blanket to trap heat.

By making and keeping in heat, cities change the weather!

A blanket of smog keeps in heat in Los Angeles.

Look for It!

Watch a local weather report on TV. Does the big city in your area have a higher temperature than small towns?

Chocolate Melt

What areas near your home get the hottest? Why?

You need:
warm, sunny day
three or more small solid chocolates—all the same size
three or more small paper plates—all the same size

1. Put each chocolate on a paper plate. Then put the plates in different spots outdoors. Here are some ideas:

- in the shade
- in a very sunny spot
- on a grass lawn
- on a sidewalk or patio
- on a fire escape

2. About 30 minutes or so later, check your chocolates. Which chocolates melted the most? Not sure? Gently push or squeeze the chocolates to see if they are soft and sticky.

3. The softest chocolates are in the warmest spots. Why might those spots be warmer than other spots?

4. Do not eat the chocolates. Throw them away and wash your hands when you are done.

Look for It!

Look at grass that grows in a sunny spot and grass that grows in a shady spot. How are the grasses different?

Hot-Air Spinner

Where can you feel hot air rising?

You need:

paper	scissors
pencil	tape
thread	

1. Trace or copy the pattern on page 9 onto paper and cut it out.

2. Tape the end of a thread to the center.

3. Hold the spinner by the thread above a warm spot. Some ideas:

- sunny windowsill
- running TV, computer, dishwasher, or other machine
- hood of a garaged car that just stopped running

4. Does the paper spin? If so, hot air is rising and pushing the paper. Moving air, hot or cold, is called wind.

5. On a very calm day, use your Hot-Air Spinner outdoors. Hold it above a brick, stone, or concrete walkway, for example. Where else might your spinner spin?

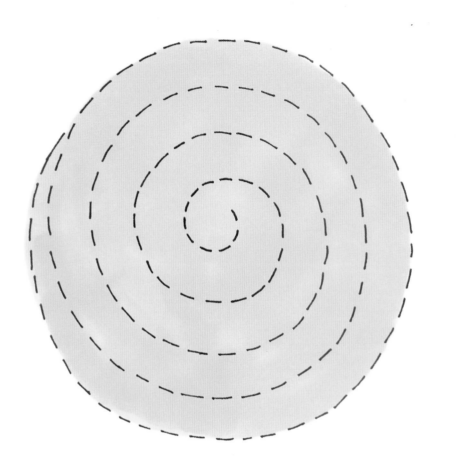

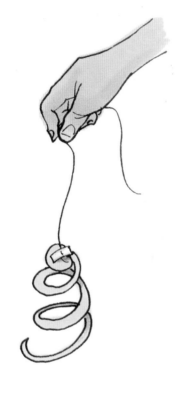

Look for It!

In cities, rising hot air can make bits of paper go up instead of fall down.

Chapter 2

A Wind-Powered School

Spirit Lake, IA. — A strong wind, such as a tornado or hurricane, can blow over a tree. But wind power can do good things, too. It can power houses, farms, and, in one town, a whole elementary school!

Spirit Lake Elementary School in Spirit Lake, Iowa, has a wind turbine (TER-bine), a very tall machine with blades.

Wind pushes the blades, making them spin. The spinning blades turn gears, round machine parts, inside the turbine. The turning gears cause a gadget called a generator to make electricity. A cable carries the electrical power into the school.

One wind turbine makes enough electricity to power the whole school. Imagine what hundreds or thousands of wind turbines can do!

In some places in California and Hawaii, wind turbines help to power whole cities. For wind turbines to work, the wind does not have to blow hard. But it does have to blow often. Could a wind turbine work in your area?

One wind turbine powers all the lights and other electrical devices at Spirit Lake Elementary School, Iowa.

Look for It!

You cannot see wind. But you can see wind push things: tall grass, leaves, flowers, flags, dust, and clothing.

Wind Flappers

Does wind blow often in your area? Where?

You need:

tissue paper	thread
pencil	tape
scissors	5-by-7-inch card or old greeting card

1. Cut a piece of tissue paper the same size as the card.

2. Fold the paper in half and tape it shut. Then cut fringes at the bottom. Open the Wind Flapper so that it is round.

3. Use the pencil to punch one small hole in the top of your Wind Flapper. Put a piece of thread through the hole and tie it in a knot. Now, decorate your Wind Flapper. Make as many Wind Flappers as you like.

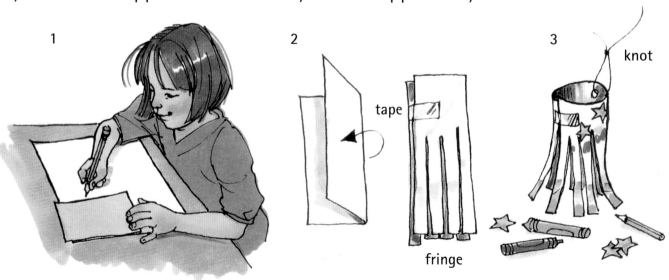

1

2   tape   3   knot

fringe

4. On a non-rainy day, tie or tape your Wind Flappers to objects. Some ideas:

- a low tree branch
- the corner of a building
- the side of a building
- the handlebar of a bike
- a porch or deck post

5. Wind makes Wind Flappers flap and flutter. Which ones are in very windy spots? Is the wind steady or does it blow in gusts?

6. Does wind blow inside your home? Use Wind Flappers to find out!

Look for It!

Wind socks are big, long bags that catch the wind. They show pilots which way the wind is blowing.

Breezy Bubbles

How can you tell which way the wind is blowing?

You need:
bubble juice and wand
an open area outdoors

1. Blow bubbles straight out in front of you. Bubbles float the same way the wind is blowing. Which way is the wind blowing now? Does it change direction?

2. Blow two batches of bubbles, one above your head and another near your knees. Do the high and low bubbles float in the same direction?

3. A steady wind makes bubbles float smoothly. Gusts make them bob up, down, and around. Is the wind calm, steady, or gusty today?

4. Bubbles last longer on a calm, wet day. Blow bubbles upward. How many seconds do the bubbles last in the air? Count each second as, "One bubble-mania, two bubble-mania, three bubble-mania," and so on.

5. Blow bubbles on a different day. Do they last longer or shorter this time?

Chapter 3

Catching Fog

El Tofo, Chile — Fog is a cloud near the ground. Like sky-high clouds, it is made of tiny drops of water.

In the mountain town of El Tofo, Chile, in South America, people "catch" the water drops in fog. They use "fog water" to drink and to water plants!

How do they "catch" fog? With fog catchers, of course. Fog catchers are big nets with tiny holes. Each net is as wide as a garage.

Wind pushes fog through the holes in the nets. Tiny water drops stick to the nets. More water drops join them, forming bigger drops. Soon, the drops are big enough to roll down the nets into a bucket.

Would a fog catcher work in your area? You need lots of fog and a steady wind. Fog is common on mountaintops and cities near the sea.

In El Tofo, Chile, giant nets trap and collect the water drops in fog.

Look for It!

This is frozen fog! It is called rime. Rime forms when tiny water drops in fog freeze and stick to objects.

Fog in a Bottle

How can you make fog?

You need:
plastic soda bottle (empty, no cap)
hot water
ice cube
flashlight (optional)

1. Fill the soda bottle with hot water. Let it sit for a few seconds.

2. Pour out almost all of the water. Leave about an inch of water on the bottom of the bottle.

3. Right away, hold an ice cube on top of the bottle. Wait a few seconds for the bottle to "cloud up" with fog. To see the fog better, turn out the lights and shine a flashlight through the bottle.

4. How else can you make fog? Some ideas:

• On a cool, rainy day, sit in a car with the doors and windows closed. Your hot breath can fog up the windows.
• On a very cold day, breathe out. Your breath might freeze into a cloud of ice fog, or fog made of tiny ice crystals.
• On a hot day, open a freezer. A cloud of ice fog might float out. Feel the air just below the freezer. Does it feel cold? Cold air sinks.

1" of hot water

Look for It!

On a foggy day, shine a flashlight into the fog. How far does the beam reach? Is all the fog the same thickness?

Jet Clouds

Can you tell when it is about to rain? How?

You need:
a sunny day
a place where jets fly overhead

1. Watch for a contrail in the sky. A contrail is a fluffy, white line made by a jet. The line is a cloud made of bits of ice, or frozen water.

2. Watch the contrail for a few minutes. How does it change?

3. If the contrail disappears in a few minutes, the sky is dry. If the contrail lasts more than 20 minutes or so, the sky is wet. A wet sky is a sign of rain. How long do today's contrails last? Do you think it will rain soon?

4. Keep watching and timing jet contrails on different days. With practice, you can use them to forecast rain!

Look for It!

Contrails look like cirrus (SEER-us) clouds, which are light and feathery. Both contrails and cirrus clouds form very high in the sky.

Chapter 4

Lightning Sparkers

Gainesville, FL — The state of Florida is the lightning capital of the United States. More lightning strikes there than any other state.

Scientists flock to Florida to study lightning. They also go there to spark lightning, or make it happen.

The scientists do not make lightning out of thin air. They wait for a storm to fill the skies. The storm makes lightning here and there. But the flashes come and go very quickly. Scientists are never sure exactly where to look.

To make lightning strike in a certain spot, scientists launch a small rocket into the storm. A long, thin wire trails the rocket. Often, nothing happens. But once in awhile, the rocket and wire cause an electric spark to form. That spark is lightning!

The lightning lasts for just a split second. But scientists can take a picture of it because they knew where to point the camera ahead of time.

Scientists in Gainesville, Florida, used a rocket and a wire to make lightning spark.

Look for It!

All lightning makes thunder, loud booms and rumbles. So why do you sometimes see lightning, but hear nothing? It's too far away for the sound to reach you.

Homemade Lightning

Have you ever felt a little spark?
If so, what were you doing at the time?

You need:
a dry, cool day
wool carpet or rug
pet cat (long-haired, if possible)
fresh laundry in a dryer

You can "spark lightning" in your home! These experiments work best on a cool, dry day. If you do not feel sparks, wait for another day and try again.

1. Walk on a carpet in your shoes. Shuffle your shoes to rub them against the carpet. Touch a metal object such as a doorknob. Feel a shock? That shock is like a tiny spark of lightning!

2. Rub a friendly cat, back and forth. Do you feel little shocks or hear little crackles? "Mini-lightning"!

3. On laundry day, wait for the dryer to finish. Open the door and let the clothes cool for a full minute. Put the clothes in a basket and scramble them. If clothes stick together, pull them apart quickly. The little electric shocks and crackles are homemade "lightning"!

Look for It!

During a thunderstorm, look out a window for lightning. As soon as you see a flash, close your eyes. Look for an image of the flash on the inside of your eyelids!

Chapter 5

Iceberg Harvest

Newfoundland, Canada — Icebergs are chunks of ice that float in cold seas. They can be as big as houses, apartments, and even whole cities!

Seawater is salty. But the ice in an iceberg is fresh, frozen water. People in deserts and other dry places need that freshwater. They do not get enough rain.

Here is the problem: Icebergs form in the far north and far south. People who need water live far away from those polar regions. How could you harvest, or collect, icebergs and move them before they melt into the sea?

A company in Canada grabs chunks of icebergs with a crane. The crane drops the chunks onto a ship. The ice melts in a heated room. Then the ship takes the iceberg water to a factory, where it is put into bottles.

Bottled iceberg water is very costly. So Peter Quilty, a scientist in Australia, has another idea. He wants to harvest a whole iceberg, not just chunks.

Quilty's plan is to wrap an iceberg in plastic to keep the ice from melting quickly. A ship would then tow the berg on a rope to a dry area such as North Africa. Part of the iceberg would melt, but not all of it.

A company in Newfoundland, Canada, collects fresh frozen water from an iceberg.

©Darlene Mulcahy White

Look for It!

Most of an iceberg is below the water. Float an ice cube in a glass. How much of the cube is above water?

Melt-a-thon

How can you keep an ice cube from melting quickly?

You need:
two or more ice cubes
egg carton or fast-food containers (clean and empty)
materials to keep ice from melting (see step 1)

1. What materials might keep ice from melting? Some ideas:

- plastic wrap or plastic sandwich bag
- fabric scraps
- aluminum foil
- sawdust
- lard, shortening, or butter
- packing materials such as bubble wrap or packing peanuts

2. Cover one ice cube with your choice of material. Put the ice cube in an egg carton section or fast-food container.

3. Put a second ice cube in another egg carton section or container. Do not cover it with anything.

4. Do you want to test more ideas? If so, wrap other ice cubes in materials. Put each one in its own egg carton section or container.

5. Close the lids and set the containers in a sunny spot for several hours. Open the lids and compare the cubes. Which ones melted the least?

Look for It!

Salt makes ice melt. That is why cities put salt on icy roads in winter.

See-through Cubes

Ice cubes can be clear, white, or a little of both.
How can you make a clear ice cube?

You need:
ice cube
tap water
two ice cube trays
two bowls

1. Look closely at an ice cube. Does it look white? If so, the cube is full of tiny air bubbles. What part of the cube is whitest?

2. Slowly pour hot tap water into an ice cube tray. Set the tray in a warm place for a couple of hours.

3. Quickly pour warm or cold tap water into a second tray.

4. Put both trays in the freezer overnight.

5. Empty the trays into separate bowls. Which cubes are clearer?

Is the ice on a pond clear, white, or a bit of both?

A Few Words About Weather

cloud: a bunch of very small water drops

contrail: the long, white cloud that jet planes sometimes make as they fly

fog: clouds near the ground

freeze: change from liquid to solid, such as water freezing into ice

glacier: a huge, frozen river that flows very slowly downhill

gust: sudden blast of wind

ice: frozen water

iceberg: a chunk of glacier that breaks off and falls into the sea

lightning: very hot electric sparks in the sky

melt: change from solid to liquid, such as ice melting into water

pollutants: unwanted or harmful chemicals, such as smoke or smog in the air

thunder: the sound that lightning makes

thunderstorm: any storm that makes lightning and thunder